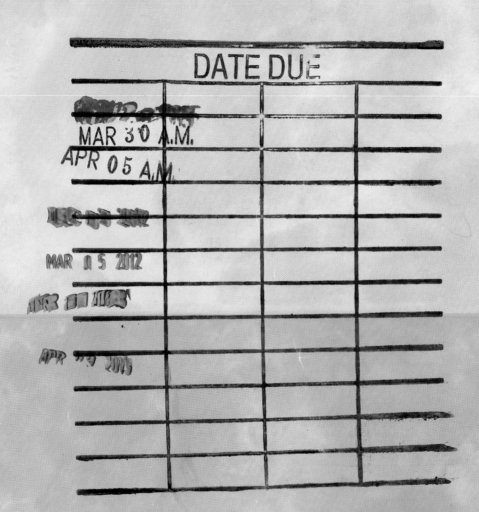

DATE DUE

MAR 30 A.M.			
APR 05 A.M.			
DEC 13 2012			
MAR 05 2012			
APR 01 2013			
APR 19 2013			

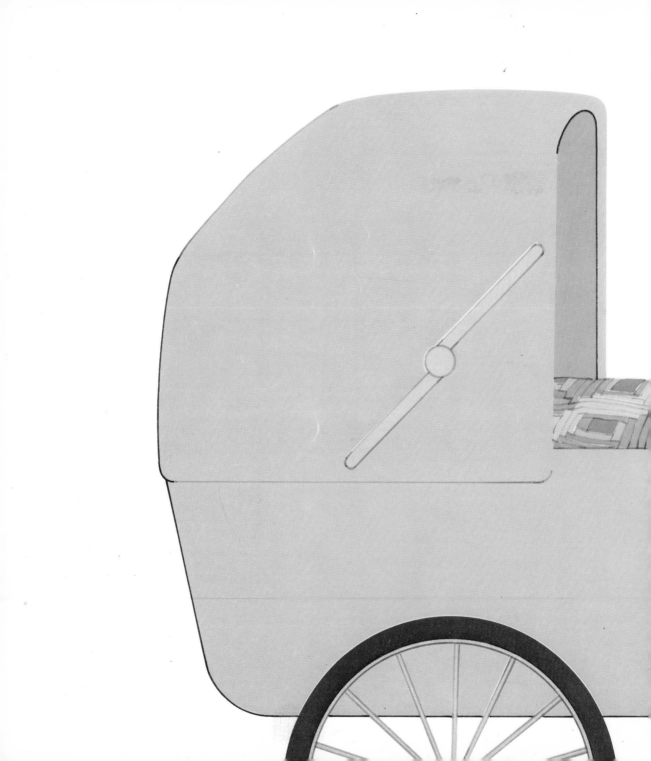

When You Were a Baby

Ann Jonas

Greenwillow Books/New York

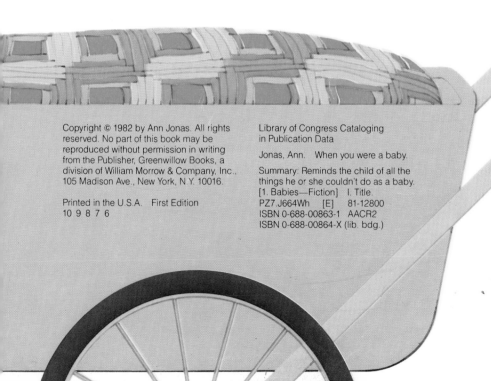

Library of Congress Cataloging in Publication Data

Jonas, Ann. When you were a baby.

Summary: Reminds the child of all the things he or she couldn't do as a baby.
[1. Babies—Fiction] I. Title.
PZ7.J664Wh [E] 81-12800
ISBN 0-688-00863-1 AACR2
ISBN 0-688-00864-X (lib. bdg.)

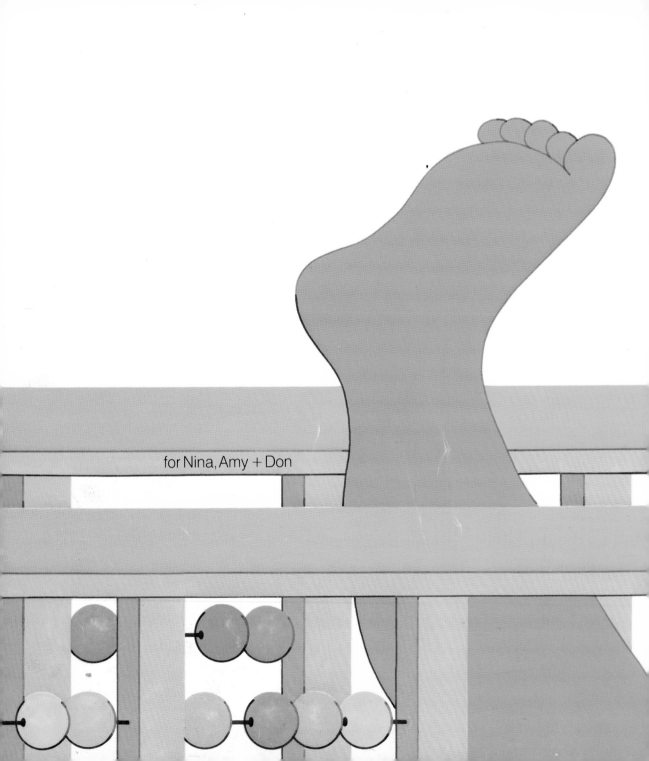

for Nina, Amy + Don

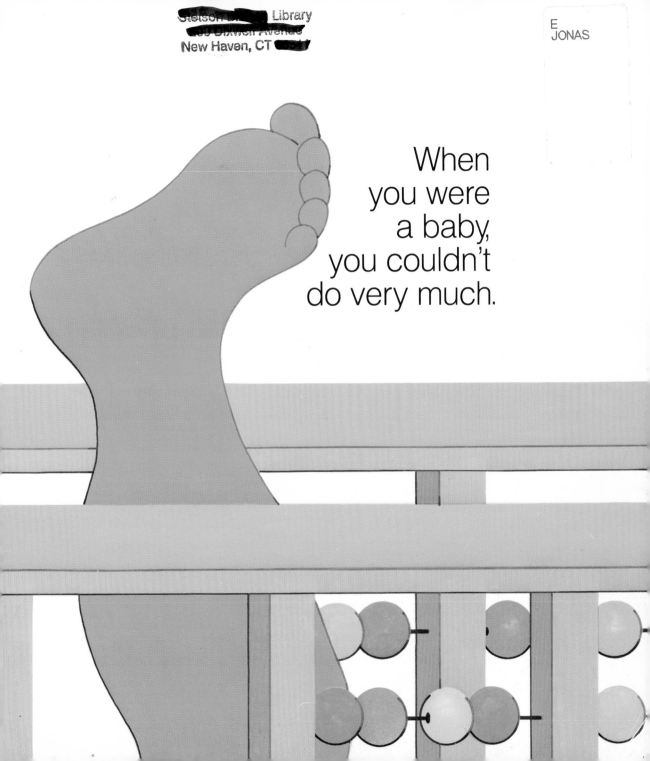

When
you were
a baby,
you couldn't
do very much.

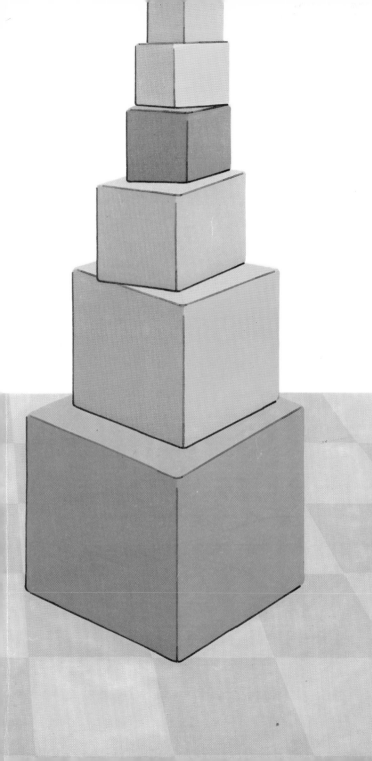

You
couldn't
pile
your
blocks
so high,

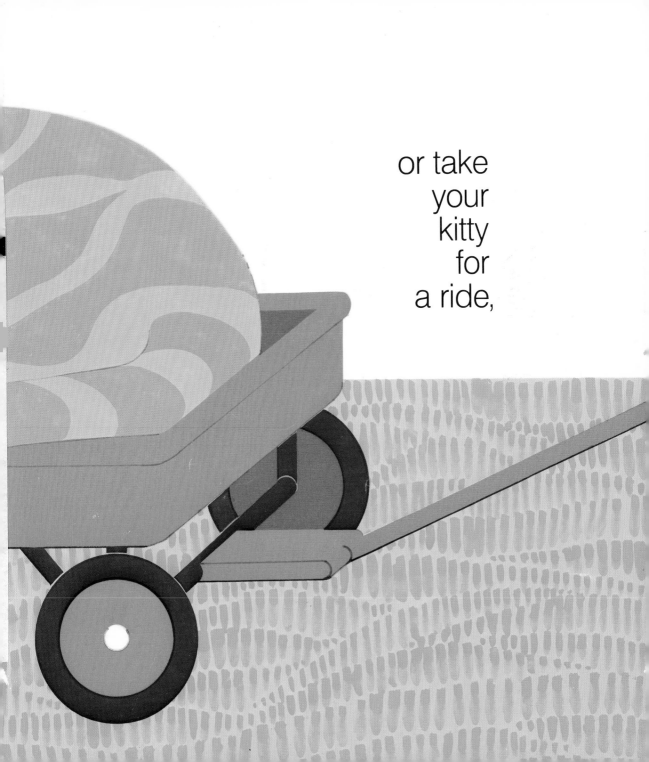

or take
your
kitty
for
a ride,

or splash
in puddles
in your
new boots.

You didn't drink
from a glass
or eat
with a spoon.

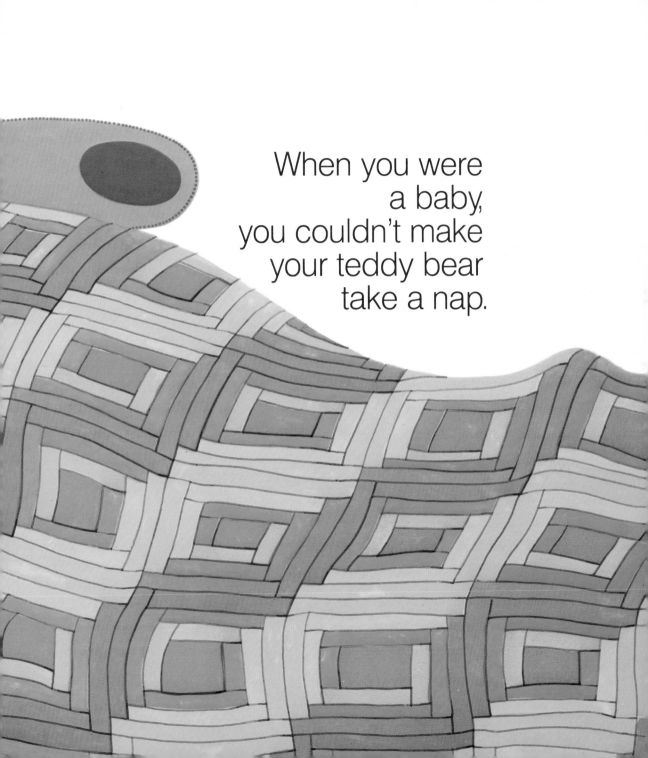

When you were
a baby,
you couldn't make
your teddy bear
take a nap.

You couldn't
roll your ball
across the floor,

or sail boats
in the bathtub.

When you were a baby,
you couldn't
teach your doll
to sit in a chair,

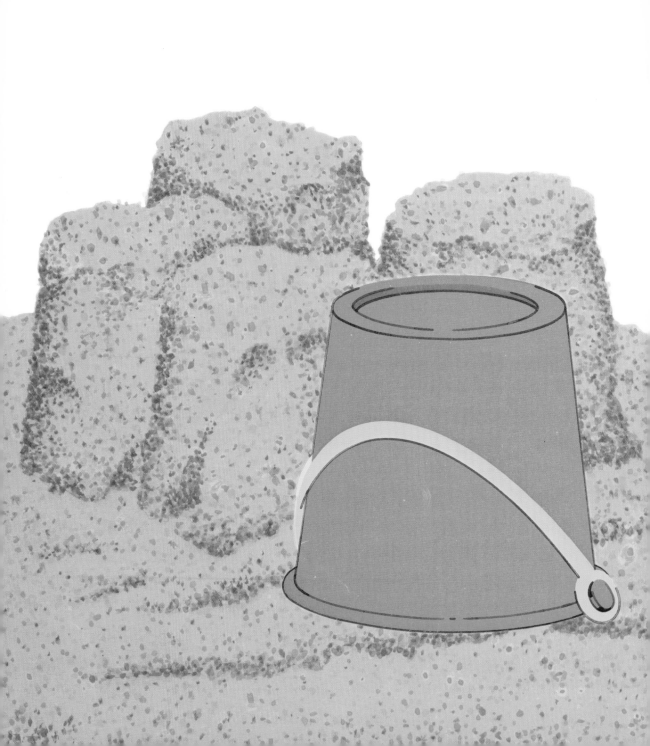

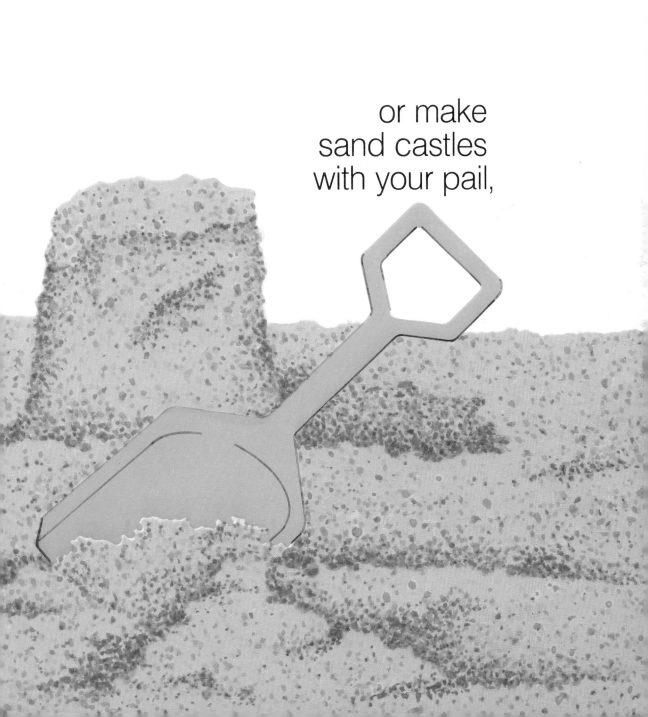

or make
sand castles
with your pail,

or take your dog
for a walk.

But now you can!